How to trade a currency fund

Jarratt Davis

ISBN: 1466279451
ISBN-13: 9781466279452

LCCN

DEDICATION

All of my adult life has so far been focused on working for myself and enjoying the freedom and flexibility that this brings, most of that time has been spent with the industry of Forex trading. Many of the people that I have met on this journey have been influential in molding me and my decision making process along the way.

This book is dedicated to my closest family, without whom I would never have even dreamed my dream, let alone live it.

CONTENTS

ACKNOWLEDGMENTS

There were a few key influential people that helped me either with their words or with their actions.

Anthony Wood is the person that gave me my first real break in trading, and let me loose on tens of thousands of dollars of his own money to give me a shot.

Rob Pampling gave me my first chance to trade at an institutional level, for his Fund, and for that chance and experience I will be eternally grateful.

Vic Jung and Peter Bain made room for me at their training and education company, and allowed me to share my experience and refine my training methods on their fantastic client base.

I'd like to mention my hundreds of students, many of which are still close friends and trading partners, for helping me develop myself as a trader and an educator.

I would also like to thank the hundreds of individuals that I have met on my adventures who have played a part in my success, and been there for my failures.

1 WHY WE TRADE

The phone rang out twice before I managed to put down my drink and answer it; it was a conference call with my Fund manager and the owner of the brokerage house that we were trading through. As I sat there listening to the nuances of slippage and bank feeds I looked around and realized that I was sat in a hotel lobby, in a permanently warm climate, sipping a cocktail at 2pm in the afternoon...

What was even better is that I had just received my commissions from last month's trading and was now truly able to live wherever I wanted, whenever I wanted. Later that day I would take a stroll along the beach and find a letting agent that could find me a nice apartment with a pool, overlooking the ocean. This is exactly why id started trading in the first place, the freedom to live wherever I wanted, whenever I wanted to.

The journey had seemed so long and hard, it had taken me around 2 years from the time I first heard about Forex to the time I was trading professionally for a living, which doesn't sound like much in hind sight, but at the time was one of the toughest times of my entire adult life. At one point I was living back at home, and eking out an existence each month on what most people in the western world would consider an average wage for a single days work.

I didn't want to get a full time job because I knew that once I was in that cycle I would get comfortable and probably end up losing sight of my goal of becoming a professional trader. I needed to focus every day and continue my learning.

I would spend on average 18 hours a day at the screens absorbing as much information as I possibly could, trying to find a system that would give me consistent winning trades and boost my account size exponentially. I joined forums, and basic education websites where basic trading concepts were discussed at great length and I would experiment with various different strategies that I hoped would bring me the gold at the end of the rainbow.

I was searching for something that would allow me to turn the screens on each morning and make profitable trades on a regular basis, I knew that I couldn't win all my trades of course, but certainly the majority of them should be profitable. As all of this was taking place I was living off the savings generated from my previous business, which I had sold the year before, and doing some part time work on the side to top up my income from time to time.

All the while, people around me were telling me that trading was a mugs game, and that it's impossible to make any consistent returns over time. At one point I was told to just give up and get a "proper job" because trading clearly wasn't working and was probably never going to work. This particular comment stayed with me ever since and was probably one of the driving factors that powered me through those dark days.

The funny thing is, people were now saying how lucky I was and how they wish they could do what I do, and this always makes me smile, because luck had nothing to do with it.

This is the story of my own journey, but mainly it's a detailed guide to becoming a fund trader and trading other people's money, not only how to do it but where to look for investors, how to select your broker, and what kind of experience / qualifications you need or don't need in order to do it. I will also go into details about things most people, including myself, didn't even consider until they were faced with the problems that they presented. Intertwined in all these lessons is the story of how I went from running my own cleaning business to trading 10 million dollars at a time in the Forex markets.

My aim with this book is to give you the blue print for doing the same thing; if that is the path you wish to follow, except you will have the steps that actually lead you there clearly laid out ahead of you. It is not padded out with useless fluff, it is short, straight to the point and contains things that you can take away and actually use.

But before we get to that, there are a couple of major issues that constantly get thrown at me, so we will get those out of the way first:

Isn't trading a zero sum game? If someone makes money someone else loses how can this provide a consistent income?

Every business involves people competing against each other for a finite piece of the pie, with the winners making money and the losers going broke. That's the sad state of our economic system. Trading is simply a more efficient version of that, which is why you will never have a 100% winning accuracy. One thing to bear in mind with trading though, unlike most competing markets, is that not everyone in the currency markets are speculating for pure profit, in fact a vast section of the market is trading for other reasons, like genuine currency exchange, for holiday money, staff wages abroad, the implementation of economic policies, and the list goes on...

This creates opportunities as the prices move up and down which speculative traders can take advantage of.

The fact is if you follow some simple steps you can make consistent profits.

But I don't have any financial qualifications; I never worked in a bank

These are all things we have in common; I dropped out of college, got mediocre grades at school and would never ever be considered a suitable candidate according to current bank hiring protocol.

However, the fact remains that I still managed to pull it off, without any kind of guide or book... Just by reading this, you are already 2 steps ahead of me when I first started.

If I can do it, so can you.

If you can trade successfully why did you even want to trade other people's money, or teach people how to do it anyway? ... Why not just grow your own account and get quietly rich?

This is probably one of the most common questions that gets thrown my way, and always makes me smile, because it almost always comes from someone with totally warped expectations of trading.

The fact is that trading is a business that must be taken seriously, like we already mentioned it is a perfectly efficient market where niches come and go rapidly and everyone is competing to make the same available profits, this means that super high returns are either impossible to achieve or impossible to sustain without massive risk, and remember the old saying 'the house always wins' so if you have super success but continue to take the risk you will eventually lose it all.

Therefore, the appropriate way to trade consistently for a living is to find a niche, but trade at very low risk and exposure, so that if the niche does cease to exist, you haven't blown your life savings. Trading for a fund gives you access to high amounts of capital which means that you can make lots of money but in terms of your overall capital the risk is still very small.

Teaching other people how to do the same, providing you are skilled enough and possess the ability to both trade and teach competently, also gives another revenue stream which is stable and consistent, it won't make you rich, but if that is your goal, it will be quite a few years down the line before you can comfortably turn away and extra 10 – 20k a month.

There is nothing wrong with trading other people's money or building a business teaching people how to do the same, as long as you are honest and have actually traded successfully in the first place.

2 LEARNING TO TRADE PROFESSIONALLY

If you haven't spent 20 years working on the Foreign exchange desk at Goldman Sachs or don't have a Harvard PhD in Finance then chances are, that your journey into the world of trading Forex begins at the Google Homepage.

This instantly exposes you to thousands of products and services marketed to help you make profits from Forex. However, most of those products or services are, at best, a waste of time, or at worst, an outright scam, designed to simply part you and your money as quickly as possible. So how do you know where to go for a good quality Forex Trading Education? And more importantly, what concepts should you try and learn?

Well the purpose of this book isn't to promote any particular Product or service, but rather to help you make good decisions that will bring you closer to achieving your overall goal of becoming a professional trader.

The Keys to trading consistently, can be broken down into three main categories, which, if mastered, will definitely put you among the leading contenders to find trading success.

First of all, the biggest obstacle and reason why so many new traders fail is the psychological aspect of trading. This absolutely must be addressed before you can hope to trade other people's money successfully. The bad news is that these psychological issues are amplified when under the pressure of fund management.

You must find courses and publications that will help you recognize these problems and then provide solutions to them.

Perhaps one of the very best coaches in this Field is Mark Douglas, and specifically his Book 'Trading in the zone.' This offers unique insights into how Training your mind and your view of the markets can really help your perspective on things such as losses and Draw downs. He also has a recording of a seminar available for purchase, which is just as effective at bringing home the key points surrounding trading psychology. The title is 'How to think like a professional trader' and like his book, is available from his website www.Markdouglas.com. His courses tend to be expensive, but for a very good reason, in fact it was when I took his Seminar that I really turned the corner in my own trading.

If you don't really at least understand the concept of trading psychology and why it's so important you will never make it past the hurdles that it presents. Because what most struggling traders fail to realize is that deep down at the very heart of all their trading woes are issues of psychology. Have you ever wondered why you can't seem to find a decent trading system? Or why you fear taking trades? Or why you were doing so well and then all of a sudden your account was destroyed? Or perhaps you have at one time concluded that trading is a mugs game and consistent profits are impossible?

All of these problems are a lot more common than many people realize and they are all issues of trading psychology, So make sure that you spend enough time grasping the concepts of trading and tuning your mind set to that of a professional, don't just pay lip service to this, really make a concerted effort to live and breathe it.

The second most important concept in successful trading and especially in trading other people's funds is the concept of prudent risk management. The concept of Risk management is an age old one that gets huge coverage in trading courses and seminars and books; however 95% of new traders still blow up their accounts and lose all of their money.

The reason for this is because those people are either ignorant to the importance of risk management, or worse, they only pay lip service to its merits. Agreeing that it's vital but then trading contrary to that view point. The unfortunate thing about this scenario of traders going broke through bad risk management practices is that the concepts themselves are among the simplest in trading. When I was learning to trade I never personally had a problem with risk management because I was always too worried about losing all of my hard earned money, more concerned about that, than about making my first million.

However, over the years I have met and worked with many traders and have several horror stories resulting from these people completely ignoring sound risk management principles. They include traders losing £250'000 (30% of their total equity) in a single trading session, and then making it back the following day!

These kinds of Rolla-coasters are not uncommon and can even give the impression that the trader riding them is actually on top of his game or some kind of maverick that can bend and break the rules and always come out on top. This perception is very dangerous not only to us and our own trading but to potential clients and the trader themselves, all of which will lose a lot in terms of money, credibility and future opportunities.

It's very important to just dwell on how similar we all think as human beings, which brings us back to psychology being the biggest reason why most people fail, simply because we all tend to think the same way and act the same way on those thoughts. For example, there is a very famous trader that promotes himself by sharing his trading story. The story is a true and verified one, he turned $12'000 into Almost $2 million in around 3 years.

What is your initial reaction to that statement? Do you want to go and buy his course? Does he sound like the kind of trader you want to be?

Well shortly after this amazing feat, he started his own hedge fund which did nothing but lose money and was promptly closed down after a few of years. Why? Because the original feat of turning small amounts into huge amounts was mainly luck, in those days he was risking far too much and getting rewarded for it, which is just as likely as him getting punished for it, after all on the end of every single move there is a buyer and a seller, neither of which has any real clue where the market is going next.

Of course our initial reaction to these events is usually "wow" but to a trained risk manager it's a much more disapproving tone. Generally if a trader makes huge gains against small initial investment they are considered lucky rather than talented, the only way to prove their talent is through time, and unfortunately there do not exist many traders, even the most famous ones, that didn't eventually go broke through their trading.

With that in mind it's absolutely critical that you focus your energy on learning and more importantly implementing sound risk management principles.

Risk management is not usually something that you have to pay a lot of money for in terms of education, in fact these days the internet is littered with articles and coaches that will happily train you in the arts, for very little cost, if any at all.

Although, I did learn a massive lesson in how most novice, investors and traders view risk management, and how that view point can cost people entire life savings...

I had been trading quite successfully for around 6 months, but still had no trading capital or income...However I found a new website which allowed me to give my trading signals to other traders that just wanted to follow someone else that made profit.

The site was called www.GFsignals.com and still exists to this day, although when I first started trading through them, they had far fewer traders and the competition was much lower.

It was a very simple process, each week I would input my trade calls into the website and anyone that chose to subscribe could follow my trades. At the end of each week the results would be posted and the top performers would stand out and get more subscribers whilst the poorer performing traders fell to the bottom of the pile and so on.

At the peak of my trading signals service I had over 30 subscribers each paying $150 for my trades, which meant that by the time the signals company had taken their cut I was making over $3000 per month for effectively trading a demo account.

This income from my trading signals allowed me to remain at home in front of the charts, which in turn allowed me to continue my education and focus on even more profitable strategies, because, despite the fact that I was making regular pips, the way I was doing it was totally unsustainable, and if combined with poor risk management would almost certainly result in an utter disaster, as I was about to discover...

I had been sending my signals for almost six months, and had been consistently one of the top performing traders, making a very consistent income from my subscriptions. This income even allowed me to open a very small live trading account from which to start my journey to professional trader.

One day however, something happened that completely altered my perception of trading and more importantly taught me how other traders are usually totally unprepared, and that risk management is a truly vital piece of the trading puzzle.

My method at the time was based on higher timeframe trading and waiting for a currency pair to start moving away from either an overbought or an oversold situation.

I would scan the pairs each night, at the close of the day and identify the pairs that were ready to start moving either up or down, and would then place my trades, with a time based stop loss covering the whole day and take profit levels the same, which meant that I would basically leave all positions open until the same time next day and collect my pips.

The principle at the time was that any losing trades would be covered by the winning trades, and because all trades that were entered had a slightly higher chance of going my way than against me.

What I failed to realize, was that the traders following me would decide after a few weeks of success to ramp up their leverage and risk exposure.

Looking back and for you reading this, you can probably see where this is going, but at the time I was making regular consistent profits every day (at one point I was averaging around 600 pips per day!) and the method seemed solid.

So I continued, until one day it all came crashing down.

I had several open positions and a few of them started to run against me, badly, I can't remember the exact details now, but it was several hundred pips, which for me was actually ok, because I wasn't trading with any leverage, but for one particular follower, it meant his whole account got wiped out.

I still remember receiving the email, and seeing that he had lost $50'000 which was his life savings. The ironic thing was that the positions turned around and actually ended the day in small profit, but he just didn't have enough margin to sustain the drawdown, because of his over leveraging.

This experience however, was enough to make me stop dead in my tracks and re-evaluate exactly what I was doing. Yes, I was technically profitable, and yes, I made profits most days, but the fact was that if people were going to over-leverage, and blow up accounts, this was not something I could really live with.

From that day on I stopped giving exact trading signals for people to simply follow, and vowed never to do it again. If I was going to help people trade Forex I would teach them how to do it for themselves.

The other lesson I learned was that Risk management is literally the difference between life and death for your trading account.

From my own time trading, and particularly meeting and working closely with other traders, the ones that tend to last the distance, are the ones that don't make particularly spectacular returns (Due to their low risk) however the ones that do take the risk, almost always get caught out and go broke. One other common theme that I discovered was the differing attitudes to leverage, between novice Traders, educators, coaches and professionals.

A successful professional will use no leverage at all, or at least a very tiny amount (Never more than 2:1) whereas a novice trader will attempt things like risking 3% per trade and compounding their size. Again this only leads to huge losses and a shortened career, whereas avoiding leverage completely, tends to lead to smoother equity curves and more prolonged trading careers.

In fact, if I were to sum up the whole Risk management principle in one sentence it would be: "Avoid the use of Leverage" and always remember that there is no such thing as 'not enough profit'.

The final piece of the puzzle is your trading system. This should be the least of your concerns, which is why it's last on the list of things to learn, however most people make it the number one priority, which again is why most people fail.

This concept is probably the least understood by the majority of novice traders. It goes a little something like this; a trader searches high and low for a system, finds one that looks brilliant, watches it for a few trading sessions and sees its brilliance in action, and then begins live trading it, at which point its brilliance seemingly vanishes and it does nothing but lose. Then the system is dumped and the whole cycle starts again.

Sound familiar? Well that's because it's the same cycle that almost all novice traders go through. Why? Because what the trader is looking for can never be found. Most traders place the importance on the system and thus believe that in order to achieve success they must have a system that never loses or can achieve a 'hit rate' that is consistent and stable.

I myself fell into this trap at the very start of my career, and probably wasted a solid year of my time in this ridiculous, never ending cycle. However, as is often the case I encountered people who were stuck in the same cycle long before I found trading and are still trapped to this day. One person that I met and worked quite closely with in my early days was literally obsessed with developing a method that didn't lose. He became known among our group for his catch phrase, which he used when describing his system "It never ever fails"

The curious thing about him was that when I first met him, his system was supposedly bullet proof, however I managed to wipe out an entire account trading it, and every three months the entire strategy was revised or changed, and the new version was always better than the last, despite the fact that all versions "Never ever failed"

He has been in this cycle for well over 15 years, and will probably be in it forever or until he concludes that trading is a mugs game and that it's impossible to make a consistent profit, the reason? Because he has set his mind on the fact that his system is the key to achieving his dream of trading success.

So does this mean that the system is unimportant?

Well the system will be what you use to determine when to buy or when to sell and buying and selling at the right times will be key to your overall trading success. This sounds like a contradiction, "don't worry too much about your system but it's also key to your success", but it's only when we understand the nature of trading that we can truly grasp this concept.

The reason that there is little to no point in focusing solely on your trading method is that whatever you use to determine your entry into the market, will have little impact on the outcome of each individual trade, quite simply because you never know who is participating in the market or why, this explains those times when you have an absolute text book set up but the price acts as if it wasn't even there. This is even more frustrating when the last trade you took was a text book set up, and it paid, just like it was 'supposed' to.

If this happens several times (and it will, on every strategy) then the inclination is to dump the system as 'ineffective' and find a new one.

The reason that people are inclined to ditch the method and persist in the never ending cycle, commonly known as the Holy Grail quest, is because they think that to be a good trader means that you have to somehow know which way the markets will go each session that you trade, so by trading a system with this mindset they place expectations on the outcome of each trade. The expectation is, of course, that the trade should win, when in reality there is no way of possibly knowing what will happen next or where the price will go, therefore you end up with a random distribution of wins and losses which leads to disappointment which perpetuates the cycle.

The topic of how markets move and how to develop the correct view point on them is much more detailed than what I have covered here, and it's definitely a subject best left for coaches like Mark Douglas to cover, all im trying to do here is help you understand that the system really isn't the be all and end all, because it's impossible to have one that never loses.

When it comes to the strategy that you are trading, the focus should merely be; does this method result in a net gain or a net loss in my account after sustained trading? And how dramatic are the draw downs during that trading period? If the answer to the first question is yes, and the answer to the second question is not very dramatic at all, then you are onto a winner and on your way to trading professionally.

So assuming that you have taken all of that advice to heart, and are focused on merely finding a profitable strategy with no exaggerated expectation with regards to performance, where do you go to find good potential trading strategies? Well when I was learning to trade I tried almost every method and concept under the sun, but the one that caught my eye and really helped me become profitable was Support and Resistance.

If you have been trading for any length of time you have no doubt at least heard of the concept of Support and Resistance. If you haven't its very simple indeed.

Look on the price chart for an area where the price has already been repelled down, this area is now resistance, and vice versa for support. Now if price comes back to these same areas again you can be ready and sell or buy in anticipation for the price being repelled again. Of course Support and Resistance isn't quite that simple, but again the purpose of this book isn't to give trade specific education.

There are many courses on the internet that provide a detailed education on the concept of trading with Support and resistance, and my own course is just one of many. The fact is that no one course is better than another when it comes to purely informational content regarding concepts such as Support and Resistance, because the fact that these concepts exist is a fact, all that varies is the approach that one takes when trading with them.

Typing a search for 'Forex Trading System' into Google will bring up hundreds of potential trading methods that you can employ in your quest to become a professional trader.

The one thing I would say is that if you are learning from someone that has been there and done it, the education is going to be that much more insightful, as opposed to some guy that studied some charts for a few years, of which there are many!

To get you started, here are a couple of really great web sites, which offer free content: Forex-strategies-revealed.com is a fantastic resource because it literally contains every method or strategy you could possibly imagine, and along with sites like this there is lots of quality Forums where traders happily post their methods for free, one of the biggest is ForexFactory.com.

As you can see, finding a strategy is the easy part, but there is a step that most unsuccessful traders miss out completely, which, ironically is one of the keys to bringing psychology, Risk management, and your trading method together and helping you on your way to professional trading.

The step im talking about is that of testing your method.

Testing your method brings about many huge benefits that will absolutely help you become a fund trader, how? Well for a start it will give you a solid record of how your chosen system performs in real market conditions, this is very important for two reasons, firstly, you will know at the exact point your method is not performing as it should be so that you can tweak it to improve performance and secondly it will provide you with the most reliable indicator on which to base your expectations in terms of performance going forward.

Knowing that you are in the middle of a Draw down or losing streak that has happened several times before is priceless, because based on your record you will also know that every time this kind of thing has happened your system has always righted itself and continued on in overall profit.

This will help you to remain focused on the most important task at hand, taking the next trade. If you didn't have this data the most likely scenario is that you would see the losing streak as another failed system and dump it in search of a 'better' one.

So again find a course or coach that helps you carry these steps out, I don't do personal coaching but I do have my Forex trading course which basically outlines everything that I did which worked, whilst leaving out all the things that didn't, I also outline in much greater detail the testing process that almost every other 'guru' seems to miss out.

But again, no one course or coach or service is the be all and end all so the important thing is to find a strategy and test it to confirm that it works over a sustained period of trading, then use that history to give you the confidence to continue on trading it live. This can be done all on your own, using the resources that we have looked at in this chapter.

Through the course of this book I will reference various traders that I have met and worked with during my time, and some of those encounters involve them losing a lot of money or quitting trading altogether, simply because they didn't know or just didn't follow the principles and guidelines that I will outline here. But there have also been a few traders that have done the exact opposite, and taken what they have learned and applied it in such a way as to become fully fledged professional fund traders.

Once we have learned what we need to do, in order to trade professionally, what next?

Well the next step is all about credibility and standing out form the competition.

Learning Resources from chapter 1:

www.Markdouglas.com - Mark Douglas is the foremost expert in the field of trading psychology, on his site you can get his bestselling books, and recorded workshops that will help you grasp all of the psychological issues that all traders suffer from.

www.Learningmarkets.com – This is a free site designed to help you understand every possible aspect of trading and investing in financial markets, a very good tool to help you understand fundamental aspects of trading such as the COT report.

www.Babypips.com – This is another wonderful free resource, aimed at teaching you every basic technical concept available. It won't really help you become profitable on its own, but it will give you the knowledge base on which to develop strategies and trade plans, a must for new traders.

www.forex-strategies-revealed.com - This is an absolutely fantastic resource for finding Forex trading strategies, and best of all they are all free. Pick your favorite, prove it works, and then trade it!

www.forexfactory.com – Probably the largest of all the Forex sites out there

3 BUILDING CREDIBILITY

In my various roles as a trader, coach and consultant I get exposed to a wide array of different people within the industry. And one of the most common questions that im asked is 'how do I trade for a fund'?

The people who ask me this question are usually well versed in trading education, and have traded every concept imaginable, and many of them have even found a certain level of success in what they do to the point where their next goal is to trade for other people, and leverage their ability to make money from the markets. The replies I give to this question are always the same, trade for 6 – 12 months and create a consistent track record demonstrating low risk, small Draw downs and above average returns, once they have this record I advise them to get the track record audited by an independent third party and then get back to me. The reason for this answer, is that anybody can produce amazing looking trading statements, freshly printed, and freshly photo-shopped (call me cynical)

In fact, one of the major reasons I decided to take the act of trading myself seriously was because I seriously over estimated the amount of people that could actually trade consistently, and profitably. If ever there was a perfect niche where demand out stripped supply it was in the world of currency fund trading.

When I first started trading, I became a member of several forums and chat rooms, and it was through one particular room that I met a trader that told me all about his success, and offered to help me get there too. Of course this was fantastic, and he gave me live presentations and showed me step by step how he traded and how to enter and exit the market etc... In fact to this day he is one of the greatest technical traders I have ever seen. He eventually suggested that we work together. He had credibility with me.

The structure of the partnership was simple, he would do the trading and I would go off with the trading statements that he provided and find him clients. We would then split the performance fee each month 50 / 50. Now this seemed like a very good deal, and my naïve greedy younger self could see huge potential from this 'business'. For a start he was averaging 30% a month, which was just incredible, I did the maths and once I had him $1 million under management I would be making an incredibly sweet income for basically nothing. I had all my angles covered, because we set it all up with the broker so that when they did the calculations at the end of each month they would automatically split it and send me my half and him his half, all the contracts were signed and sent back.

All I had to do now was go get him the clients.

At this point I was about to learn two very important lessons, first of all, *Account statements are extremely easy to fabricate,* and secondly, *a 'trader' can make a very good income from a clients account even if they lose all their money.*

The problem with my grand plan was that I was not aware of either of those two things, so I carried on regardless in the task of finding him clients. My first port of call was my own friends and family which was a very easy sell, since I already had their trust. I collected my first $50'000 account and we began the process of opening it up and getting him trading.

As I imagined all the money id soon be making for nothing, I tuned into the account viewing screen and proceeded to watch as his trading unfolded.

What I saw left me horrified, he was using huge leverage, and many times leaving positions open with no stop losses at all this made huge dents in the account equity and after just a week's trading the account, was down a massive 20%. He came up with the story of how the market had made dramatic moves, and that unexpected news had affected his position, but even though I was new, I understood that massive risk and no stops were not the hall marks of a good trader, so I closed the account and had to explain the loss to my very annoyed Friends and family, not to mention look like a total fool in the process.

I ceased finding him clients.

The one thing that kept playing on my mind though, was how could this happen, when he had such a flawless track record? And why would he trade in this reckless manner when we were making our money from performance fees? It just didn't make any sense. I discovered the answer to this mystery several years later, when I was on the road to fund trading myself, and the reason? Commission splits.

A Commission split is where you bring your client to the broker, with the intention of trading for them, and as a reward for this the broker gives you a portion of the commissions traded on that account. These commissions are charged every time a trade is placed, regardless of whether it is a winner or a loser, and are based on Volume traded. I.e. the bigger the trade size the more commissions generated. What I realised is that the reason this trader took such huge risks and experienced such large draw downs was because he really didn't care what the outcome was, only that trades were placed. He was taking a cut of the Commissions from the broker regardless of whether he made money or lost money. So in fact it was in his interest to trade bigger and bigger size, since the amount of commissions he generated was purely dependent on his volume traded.

But what about the account statements, how did he manage to demonstrate such lovely returns when his strategy was to destroy accounts? The answer to this came shortly afterward.

One very important lesson that I have learned over the years is that Forex trading as an industry tends to be a very small world, so if you develop a bad reputation it can be very difficult to hide. And conversely if you build a good reputation then you can expect some fantastic coverage and opportunities from a whole army of people eager to benefit from your status.

Due to this fact, it wasn't long before I encountered some people who had invested money with this 'trader' some much larger accounts than mine, and some with absolutely horrific out comes, for example one client lost 80% within 2 weeks, on a $100'000 account. Others lost everything.

The story was always the same, he would produce a great track record and then blow up the accounts, followed by a story explaining why this happened, some clients were even persuaded to re invest to make the money back!

It soon became quite clear that this person was not a trader, but rather a scam artist, adept at falsifying his track record and suckering clients into his web. The falsification of a track record, by the way, is about one of the easiest thing a person with low integrity can do. All it takes is a genuine account statement, which anyone can get, and then a bit of simple editing on any popular 'Photoshop' software, it is then put into a PDF format and away you go, a perfect track record.

We calculated based on the volumes he was trading and the accounts we knew about that he must have made at least $100'000 from ruining peoples accounts and taking his commission splits, no wonder he didn't mind giving me 50% of his performance fee each month, there was never going to be a performance fee to split!

The real irony was that his technical knowledge was flawless, and his skills on the price charts were out of this world, he genuinely did have a great knowledge of how to trade the markets. A lot of the skills I developed in trading support and resistance were skills I learned from him, and his 'talent' was the main reason I trusted him and started working with him in the first place.

Unfortunately he didn't possess the psychological capabilities to trade consistently or the risk management approach to protect the trading capital, coupled with the fact that he was basically a criminal.

Of course this is an obvious conflict of interest and many brokers do not allow this kind of arrangement on principle, in fact, almost no broker will now allow that kind of arrangement. However some large reputable brokers did, Dukascopy being a huge example of that, at the time. One thing to bear in mind is that even when a broker did refuse to do this there were still ways around it, for example a broker Will offer commission splits with an IB that is not a trader, so in order to get the Commissions some traders simply partner up with IB's and share the commissions, after all half is better than nothing.

Things are getting much better in the industry at the time of writing this, but at the beginning it really was the Wild West.

In an ideal world Commission splits are actually a very nice way for a trader to make a consistent income from their trading, especially in times of Draw down, because the commissions are being charged regardless of whether the trader has a share or not, so even if you don't take a cut, your trading still has to make up for them each month. And if you are an honest reputable trader, you can build a very nice structure whereby your trading income is subsidised by your share in the commissions, making the whole process much easier and a lot less stressful.

There are some brokers that actually allow this, and they simply place as many extra pips onto your client's spread as you want, and you get to keep them at the end of each month.

Of course which route you go down is entirely up to you, but it's very useful to know all of the options before you start working on your plan, and all options have their pros and cons.

The main point of this chapter is that a track record is not enough, and the only way to make a track record as close to bullet proof as possible is by getting it verified or audited.

When assessing a trader's record these days, I don't even look at it if it's not somehow verified. And when advising traders on their steps to professional fund management an audit is always a vital ingredient.

Almost every trader then replies with something like, how do I get it audited? Or what does that even mean?

First things first, an audit is simply an external check carried out by a qualified but independent third party to confirm that the results you advertise to your clients are true and actually happened. External third party means someone that isn't related to you either by blood or by business interests, and qualified means that they are appropriately equipped to make the necessary checks and reporting, for example a qualified Accountant (CPA) may be in a position to offer you the service, providing that you can encourage your broker to assist them. Or sometimes the broker themselves will be more than willing to carry out the reporting that you need to get your results verified.

The problem with audits is that there are many different types going into all sorts of different levels of detail, and it can sometimes be confusing just finding an entity that will provide a credible audit.

When I started trading for the WealthbuilderFX Hedge Fund, one of my first memories was attending a meeting with one of our European IB's in London. An IB or Introducing Broker is basically a middle man between funds and clients, taking a cut of the fees for their troubles. It was a fascinating insight into the world of professional fund management, as he explained the process of attracting new money using old track records.

One of the subjects that I found particularly interesting was that of Audited track records. For a long time prior to this I had wanted to get my small mini account history audited and verified, but couldn't seem to get anyone to take me seriously, which I obviously found irritating but after the conversation id just had, it all made perfect sense.

First of all, there are fund specific companies that carry out those kinds of tasks, companies such as Price Water house Coopers, or a company that some of the funds I worked with used, was JP Fund services, on top of this there are several types of audit, ranging from low detail all the way through to high detail, and there was also a difference in price, for example a quote for a low detail audit ran to about $10'000, and the high detail audits could be anything up to and sometimes exceeding $100'000!

The low detail audits were basically confirmation that you achieved the returns that you stated in your fund trading policy, whereas a high detail audit looked at how you achieved those returns, for example, did the traders ever breach risk management policy? Did the trader use the strategy that was outlined in the policy consistently? Or were there any deviations that a potential investor may be concerned about?

Suddenly I understood why Price water house coopers were not even interested in giving me a quote for auditing my tiny $5000 account for the previous year. The other reason that it would have been pointless at that time is because potential investors at an institutional level plant money in relation to the size of the account that you audited in the first place. So my grand ideas of walking into an office and showing my 80% annual return on a $5000 account, and walking out with $100'000 investment were a total pipe dream, the best I could expect was something more like another $5000 on top, and almost all professional investors, particularly fund managers will not invest in anything less than $100'000 chunks, and usually much more.

As I sat in the meeting and all this information was being given to me I realized that way back when I was trying to get the audit off the ground, I was looking in the wrong places for the wrong things. Instead of getting a large company to complete the audit, the best thing to do is have the broker do this for you instead. This has several benefits.

Firstly you get a verified track record for your use in attracting investors, and secondly the broker is fully aware of your performance, because after all you have been trading under their noses for the past few months. And when a private client decides to try and invest into Forex, but doesn't have the ability to trade it themselves, or the financial clout to invest in a large hedge fund, they turn to the next best source of traders, the broker.

So the broker verifying your track record will give you a certain level of credibility to a specific group of investors.

Of course, you could also use a local CPA, but the further out you get from the Trading industry the less credible your audit becomes, so if you can get your broker to carry it out, that's always preferable.

Sometimes brokers will not be prepared to do this for you, for example in Switzerland some brokers consider it a breach of privacy to open up your accounts to anyone other than you, even with your express permission. From my experience Dukascopy is one such broker that will not carry out any kind of verification. On the other hand ACM are a little bit more flexible and providing you have a decent record will offer to help you out. If you're not keen on Switzerland then the best retail broker that I ever traded with was Alpari UK, and they were also the most flexible in terms of building relationships and accommodating my needs.

The best tactic is to approach several brokers, tell them your plan and ask if they will be prepared to verify your account at a later date, and just go with the ones that agree.

The general principle when dealing with a broker in any capacity is to be aware that they firmly adhere to the adage 'you scratch my back ill scratch yours' ... So before asking for the help of a broker, you need to demonstrate that you are useful to them first. The best way to show this is by trading a live account with them, and if possible introducing friends or colleagues to trade with them too. Once you can prove your worth, a broker will tend to bend over backwards to accommodate your needs.

This is something important to bear in mind if you are planning your fund trading career from scratch.

If you are struggling to get someone to actually verify your trading accounts in the early stages, there are also several other ways that you can gain a credible verification of your account, for example sites such as MyFXbook.com and currensee.com offer to link your account to their systems, so that the whole world can look at your performance without actually having access to your account. This is a step in between you just producing an account and getting your account audited.

It may be a valuable tool for small accounts or if you don't have a few thousand lying around for a half decent audit. These sites are legitimate (at the time of writing) and offer at least some comfort for your potential clients. I love these sites and although they were not really around when I was building up my record, I have several students that have used them to great effect.

Aside from outside verification, there are several other things that you can do to gain credibility. One such thing is offering your knowledge and experience to those traders who are struggling or less experienced. This places you as an expert in your field, leading a tribe of people to where they want to be, all very good for credibility.

Educating people often has negative connotations, for example the saying 'those who can't, teach' and while this may be true for some trading educators, there are another group who see a reputation as a trading guru as something that will add to their credibility and help push them that little bit further to their end goal of becoming a professional fund trader.

At around the time I started trading successfully, I decided that helping others was a good thing to do, firstly because I genuinely liked helping others but secondly because I could see how beneficial it could be in the future.

With this in mind I set up my first trading web site, invest-fx.com, and initiated a free Skype trading chat room. On the website, I wrote out a couple of short training courses and posted them so that anyone who wanted to could learn the same things from me for free. The Skype chat room was also a freely open environment that anyone could join if they so wished. I would basically go in there each day and help other traders with their issues, and maybe point out the trades that I was taking and why etc... The chat room was an instant success, and word spread remarkably fast, until I had over 60 people in the room all interacting with me and helping each other to the common goal. Word of mouth spread via trading Forums, and the odd bit of search engine traffic but the fact was, traders were looking for an expert to help them and for those 60 people that expert was me.

Obviously 60 people doesn't sound like very many when you consider the thousands of traders all over the internet, however my two biggest opportunities in trading came as a direct result of that Skype trading room and my invest-FX website.

First of all, I met someone that was interested in my trading, so we spend quite some time going over my technique and using the concepts that had helped me up to that point. What I didn't realize at the time was that person just so happened to be a Hedge fund manager, and after a few months he invited me to join the fund and start trading for him, not bad for a free Skype chat room.

Shortly after this a large Forex training company, ForexMentor.com, discovered my room and asked if I would be prepared to offer something similar for their clients. When I did the math on the potential revenues it was a no brainer ....when we actually launched, the figures were even better than I imagined, In the first two months my new Live Trading room generated almost $100'000 in revenue.

Sadly, the time and effort that I was putting into my trading, and then my new Premium trading room meant that my Skype room got neglected and slowly died off, but I'll never forget what a huge stepping stone it proved to be, and you shouldn't rule out doing similar projects in order to gain credibility as a professional trader.

Once I was trading for the fund, we were monitored by Barclays who are probably the largest company that track the performance of hedge funds and currency funds. This again adds credibility because if your fund is being tracked then clients can trust that your trading performance is genuine, rather than using a bunch or trading statements that could easily be photo-shopped.

One final thing to consider is that of Regulation, specifically by some kind of governmental authority, for example in the UK it would be the FSA and in the US it could be the NFA, but most countries will have their independent governing bodies.

For the most traditional paths to regulation, the process is long, tedious, and expensive, not to mention the fact that Spot Forex trading is a really grey area when it comes to these bodies, they often struggle to even tell you whether regulation is even necessary, this is because, particularly in the UK Spot trading clients money via Power of attorney is not regarded as a necessarily regulated activity, for the most part the main concern of these bodies is to stop blatant scams involving 'traders' stealing investors money, which is impossible when trading Spot Forex via POA.

The reason it's impossible, is because when you trade a client's account you have no access to their money for any other reason than to trade it, and the client retains full control over the funds, allowing them to closely monitor your performance and decide for themselves when to withdraw funds or limit their exposure to your trades etc...

Therefore if you stick to your Risk management policies, it's incredibly difficult to sustain the kinds of losses that would cause any kind of legal action against you, and any losses you do sustain will be from trading pure and simple. And if there is any doubt then it is very easy for your account records and broker to verify this.

However when dealing with private clients (individual investors below $250k) one can never be too careful, to the point that if I were to offer a piece of advice regarding such clients it would be to avoid them altogether, and we will get to the reasons why shortly.

On the subject of Gaining regulation, there is a small trick that you can potentially use to get regulated quickly and almost hassle, and more importantly expense free, and for this we once again we turn to our old friend the broker.

If you form a partnership with a broker that is themselves regulated, it may be possible for you to fall under their umbrella of regulation. It obviously depends on your relationship with your broker, for example I was offered regulation with a broker if I signed up to their IB agreement, the reason I was attractive to the broker as someone who could bring them new clients was the fact that I had a small army of followers and clients that I interacted with on a daily basis, that could be promoted to.

If you talk to the broker about your plans, and make it clear that you aim to make them a lot of money in the process, through your trading of client accounts, and generating them commissions for example then you may find them more than accommodating. Of Course not all brokers will offer this, but when you're selecting your broker initially, make this one of your questions regardless.

Once you have a credible track record of trading history, including at least some kind of verification, regulation and if possible an audience of followers the next step is using it to attract trading capital.

Producing a credible track record:

www.lacrosseglobal.com – A professional Fund administration service that can help you get your accounts audited, but be prepared for the high cost.

www.acsbco.com – Another company that specializes in Auditing and administration for Hedge funds, another hefty price tag.

www.jpfs.com – Based in Europe, JPFS can help you not only with your auditing but also with getting set up as a fund.

www.myfxbook.com – This is a fantastic resource if you don't have thousands of dollars to get your initial accounts verified, you can simply connect a read only version of your trading account to this website and they will automatically keep track of your results and verify your performance. Best of all, it's free.

www.currensee.com – Similar to myfxbook, but its more social based, and they have a community of traders that you can work with and compete with. Once again it's free and gives a great third party verification of your performance.

www.Barclayhedge.com – Barclays have a very good reputation for keeping track of hundreds of hedge funds, and you can sign up with them and report your performance on a monthly basis. This is a very good way to increase credibility.

4 FINDING FUNDS

Because I was extremely fortunate to navigate my way into the path of a hedge fund manager, it may seem that my luck made my journey easy and that most people probably including yourself won't have such good fortune, and that you will have to find funds in a different way.

This is almost certainly the case, however being in the hedge fund environment, and meeting all the different types of people within the industry that I have, I am in a unique position to know about the various routes to funding, despite the fact that I didn't actually take them.

Let's return to the broker that you are trading with, previously we discussed how they may be prepared to verify your record, and that they also have access to lots of clients who are looking for someone to manage or trade their account. If planned properly this can be an excellent way to start your fund trading career, because if you broker knows your plan ahead of time then they will have you in mind when clients enquire about any Professional traders that they know of.

Getting your broker to feed you clients is about as simple as it gets, but it's often a route that goes completely unnoticed and unused by budding professional traders. This isn't the end of the opportunities though, apart from having clients that are in contact with them, they are also privy to IB's.

Remember, an IB is simply someone who introduces capital to traders, so once you have a good relationship with your broker you can start to ask about any IB's that they may be dealing with at the time, and also explore the possibility of being introduced to them.

This is basically like having your own team of Salesmen tracking down and sourcing streams of capital for you to trade. Of course this all depends on your trading performance, but if you have followed the steps of getting a solid education in how to trade professionally, your results should continue in the same manner as when you first built up your track record.

Before we go into other avenues of attaining clients funds, it's important to discuss the type of client that you need to be aiming for. In the beginning it can seem like any money is good money, however in my experience this is not the case. As with most other forms of business, generally the clients with the lowest amount of capital invested will complain the most and be the biggest drain on your time and resources.

This is due to several factors, first of all the money they have invested is usually most of their entire portfolio, despite what they claim, for this reason any Draw downs that you experience will be horrifying to them and they will want to know why it happened and when you will make it back. Remember, they have you trading their money because they can't do it themselves, which means they have an active interest in the markets and trading in general, not enough to actually trade but enough to make your life a living hell with questions and 'suggestions'.

I had several small clients like this before I started trading at wealthbuilderFX and in general, anyone investing anything below $250'000 was a waste of time and not worth dealing with.

One of my biggest lessons in this area came from the guy we looked at in chapter 1, that was obsessed on finding the 'holy grail' of trading and never taking a loss. Looking back he operated the way he did quite simply because he couldn't trade himself, it's a common story, they have great technical knowledge but they can't actually execute a trading plan consistently on real live accounts, and as we looked at earlier the main cause is poor trading psychology.

His plan was for me to trade his 'amazing system' on his money and give me a cut, which, again to my naïve young self at the time seemed a wonderful situation to get involved with.

So I absorbed his strategy and began trading it, which ended in loss after loss. At the end of each losing day he would always have some reason why the trades lost, and commend me on following the system, but give me advice on a few things I should do differently next time, until the whole of his small account was completely wiped out.

Every day he would give me new instructions, which looking back, was him just curve fitting the results to make every loser into a winner, which sadly only works in hind sight.

Eventually after almost 12 months of 'working' with him, I decided that I was effectively wasting my time and that his methods were never going to work because he simply changed them every time there was a loss, and it was this switching and inconsistency in the method that ultimately caused the accounts to perish. Of course he didn't like hearing this kind of negative comment, and proceeded to attempt to sue me for .... Theft of his money.

That's correct, he funded an account, gave me the log in details and talked me through his strategy step by step until all the money was gone, and then accused me of stealing from him...

Obviously it was ridiculous, I had all of the emails, the trading account was in his name, and no money ever exchanged hands, so the chances of me ever getting charged with criminal activity were none, but that doesn't stop that kind of event having an impact.

In the end he didn't go ahead with it and we simply went our separate ways, but if he did, then even being involved with something like that would have shaken me to the core, I am not a criminal and believe firmly that it is better to be honest above everything else... My reputation could have been completely ruined, for nothing.

Shortly after that episode, I decided that I would no longer trade for small investors and instead focus on trading for a large fund or institution somehow, the potential hassle was certainly not worth the rewards that came from trading a $10'000 micro account, and splitting the profits.

A true investor will have vast reserves of risk capital to the point where anything they have with you is nothing worth worrying about, and you won't hear a peep from them unless something really bad happens, like extreme draw down, but again, this is highly unlikely if you stick to sound Risk management principles as set out in your policy. Normal Draw down, as experienced during the time you were creating your track record will go almost unnoticed by a true investor, which allows you to get on with the task in hand, taking the next trade.

If you do decide to trade for private clients (and by private I mean below $250k investment) then id urge you to use extreme caution. Not only will they be taxing on your time and resources with their constant questions and analysis of your trades but they will also start to affect your trading psychology, causing self doubt and even fear of losing. This kind of thing can be terminal for a professional trader and anything that could even remotely cause it should be eliminated, so keep a close eye on your clients and how they are interacting with you, if it starts to get too much cut them loose, you'll be far better off for it in the long run.

One thing I employed towards the end of my time dealing with private clients was a strict non contact agreement.

For example, the agreement would state that unless certain issues arose, i.e. larger than expected Draw down was experienced on the account, then they were forbidden to contact me at any time, especially with anything trading related. If they did wish to discuss something useful, such as adding funds to their account then they should deal directly with the broker or an assistant that I had in place. All of these agreements were signed before trading began and if breached to the point of irritation, they were cut loose.

It may sound harsh or even bad business, but remember I had a client threaten to take legal action against me for theft of his money, despite the fact that I was trading via POA and accessing his money was basically impossible.

The point is, private clients are usually failed traders themselves, and as such have unrealistic expectations as to how a professional trader should perform, which means that they carry this unrealistic view point over in to other areas, such as seeing genuine trading losses as theft.

If you take one piece of advice from this chapter, avoid small, individual investors and always use a middle man if possible, this is one of the benefits of an IB. However there are plenty of negatives to IB's too...

When raising money an IB can be extremely efficient, after all it's what they do, they are linked in to all kinds of networks and capital flows. The problem comes when you begin to negotiate their fees. For the most part all IB's that I have ever dealt with have been on a performance fee cut only, which means that they get a cut of the performance fee you take from any profits that you make for your clients.

This can be on a monthly basis for the life of the account, which after a while can really become quite irritating, as the IB has done a one off deal, and now sits back while the money rolls in each month, While you are the one actually trading the money and going through all the struggles that traders typically face.

Other IB's are more reasonable and will expect either a one off fee based on a small % of the account, taken directly from the clients funds, or will simply take a one off fee, usually paid by the client, but sometimes by the trader.

Obviously our personal preference as traders is the % of the account taken at the start.

Therefore, when negotiating with IB's don't blurt out anything about monthly % cuts of performance fees until they bring it up, and when they do, act horrified, as if that is unacceptable and the end of negotiations.

Of course if the IB is a good one that can bring constant streams of Capital then it may be a noose worth having.

But that will have to be a decision you make based on all the factors, one trick I used was offering them a % of the account at the start, and then based on how much capital they raised, move up to a monthly % performance fee cut. This offers the IB incentive to work for you harder and will result in you trading larger sums faster.

Remember the better and longer your track record, and the more credibility you have associated with it, the harder bargain you can drive. Good traders are almost impossible to find, especially if we use the following definition of good trading:

'Low risk trading with small draw downs and above average returns'

Some clients may be mesmerized by the guy that made 30% last month, but trust me they are in for a painful shock sooner or later, and will either end up broke or knocking on your door to repair the damage. IB's and brokers all know this too, so if you really want to become a top trader to promote in their eyes, have that definition as your mantra.

When you possess such a record, don't be afraid to wield it, and use it to demand better deals from your IB's and your broker.

The other avenue that you can explore in terms of raising capital is that of other trading funds already in existence. Again your broker will have plenty of contacts in this department which you may be able to tap into, but remember at first you will be viewed as competition, so don't expect a warm welcome, and an abundance of helpful advice. However, if you can use your record to show them that you are a talented trader and that you are keen on using that talent to trade their funds then you could be in with a shout.

There are basically two approaches you can take to existing funds; firstly you can approach them with the possibility of becoming a trader for them. And secondly you can propose that they diversify some of their portfolio to you.

If you're contacting them through a broker then chances are that they will be a currency trading fund already and won't be keen on diversifying with you, mainly because you're doing the exact same thing as them, so it's not really diversification at all.

The best approach for this is as a potential trader for the fund, chances are they are already set up, and won't need you, but if your record is better than theirs you may get something from them.

If your record is indeed better than theirs, why would you want to trade for them, rather than attracting your own money?

Well the main reason is that they are already established and can probably set you up with $1million to trade quite easily, which is going to be a task for you to achieve based on the fact that most investors look to invest what the trader has already been trading based on the track record. Therefore, unless you have been building your record on a $1million account, your initial investments are going to be significantly lower.

Even if they don't have any positions at that time, it's good to be on their radar, and the more funds you approach the better your chances of finding one open to you.

The other approach, involves moving away from your broker, and onto third party fund rating companies. For example Barclay's, are a company that tracks hundreds of different funds of all sizes and shapes, and then passes this information on to investors. Therefore if you want access to hundreds of hedge funds this is a great place to start. It's a premium service, but the contacts you could generate here are potentially worth infinitely more than any subscription charge you will pay.

This kind of place will have a wider ranging array of fund, many of which will be looking for places to diversify into, and you could just be what they are looking for, remember though, these kind of funds don't invest anything less than $100'000 chunks (often a lot more) so you may have to get your timing right before approaching them.

Remember, the closer you get to trading larger funds the better quality your client, however, to reach this stage could take time and you need to be prepared to build up your trade size slowly. On the other hand, people are generally greedy, so if they see your performance and like it, you could end up with a lot of money in a very short space of time, so it's worth preparing for this eventuality also.

Because of my own experience and reputation in the industry, one of my roles is consulting to start up funds on how to successfully build up a team of traders that would be stable and produce consistent returns each year. My unique position as trader, coach and consultant have privileged me to almost every angle in the trading world, and I have a pretty good idea what makes a good trader and how to go about building a team from the ground up.

Personally I have no problem recommending people that have no experience trading large volume as long as they demonstrate that they can stick to their pre defined strategy, and replicate their track record results on a small account for us, we then incrementally increase the amount they trade until they were up to full size.

The point of this is that if you can find smaller start up funds these have all the resources required to attain funding, whilst being flexible enough to give you a shot, these opportunities are rare but it's good to know they exist.

Resources for locating investment

http://www.cfhmarkets.com/ - CFH markets are a London based Broker that deal only with institutional investors. This means that they have access to hundreds of clients, IB's and small trading funds that could potentially take you on. These guys are a great resource if you are looking for a helpful broker with good contacts.

www.ac-markets.com – ACM are a Swiss broker, with a more retail back ground, which may be helpful if you are currently only trading a small account, however they also have access to IB's and clients that you could tap into when the time is right. They are also much more helpful than many brokers when it comes to helping you get off the ground with finding clients etc...

www.Linkedin.com –This is a very useful place to find IB's and fund managers that you can connect with and build up lasting partnerships. I have had a lot of opportunities presented to me through this portal.

www.Barclayhedge.com – Again, we looked at these in chapter 1, but they can be very useful for locating funds which you can network with and contact.

5 PROFESSIONAL TRADING

Once you have found your path into fund trading initially, there are a whole host other of surprises and lessons to be learned. The lessons I learned here are quite useful and can save you time and more importantly money.

One of the first questions you may be wondering is how much do traders make? The answer to this question is truly dependent on the type of fund or organization that you work for, for example a behemoth corporation such as Goldman Sachs may offer their traders a basic salary, plus bonuses based on how they perform.

At the other end of the scale a new trader that has recently ventured onto their own, and accepted the first batch of client accounts to trade will most likely be on a performance fee only scale, i.e. if they don't perform they don't eat.

There are medium areas, for example we looked earlier at the possibility of being on a Commission split with your broker, which would at least provide a steady stream of something to complement your trading. Other operations, small funds for example run the method of charging an annual fee, plus performance fee.

This has the same effect of stabilizing the income so that cash flow is at least calmer than the brutal performance fee only model that I spent most of my early days on.

If you are singularly focused on trading then there are several options when looking for different streams of income, and I wouldn't rule any of them out. Just because certain models can be abused by dishonest individuals, doesn't mean that they should be avoided by those of us who don't intend to fleece our clients.

Outside of trading, we already looked at the benefits and possibilities of becoming a recognized expert in the field of trading, because let's face it, if you have made it this far you are far better off than most people attempting the same thing, and almost certainly have something valuable to offer them in terms of expertise or information.

One of the most common 'snipes' I receive from people who look at the fact that I also train others to trade, is "If you're so good at trading, then why are you bothering to teach others, why not just go and get rich trading?"

The answer is short, simple and to the point; because I make a lot of money from it.

When I reach a point in my life when I can happily turn my nose up at $10'000 - $30'000 per month that my training generates, then I will, until then, I'll take it.

I have a colleague that also runs a fund, but does training courses and seminars as well. He has built himself a solid reputation in the industry, but he is by no means selling out stadiums. The fact is, you don't need a vast army of thousands following you and buying your expertise, he runs seminars several times a year, and charges $1500 per head, for a one / two day event. He usually gets around 30 people in attendance at that price. This initially sounds hardly worth bothering with, but then you calculate the amount of money this is worth and realize that $45'000 for a weekend isn't actually that bad after all. Two or three of these a year and you have yourself a solid income aside from trading. This obviously takes all the pressure off, but at the same time isn't so time consuming as to distract you from the ultimate goal of trading people's money, because conducting a few small seminars a year certainly won't make you rich, but trading hundreds of millions of dollars will.

So always remember, to keep the priority trading, but if you can offer something from an educational point of view, that doesn't take up all your time, then go for it!

There are literally hundreds of other avenues aside from trading, where you can explore the concept of earning a residual income whilst continuing to build you track record. The fact is, that to be trading the kind of volumes you need in order to be making Ferraris every month you are going to need a sustained, verified, record on large accounts. This is very time consuming, because you can't just build up a steady record over night, and getting audits conducted can be extremely expensive, especially if your broker offers no assistance in this.

Let's look at some calculations to bring this home.

Trading account value $1million

Average Performance each month 2% - this is a very good return, and achievable inside our mantra of good trading.

Monthly profit = $20'000

Traders performance fee 30% = **$6'000**

$6'000 is certainly not bad, for a month's income, however bear in mind that next month you may enter Drawdown, and take home nothing, and then the month after you have to recover to your previous high before making any more money. This is suddenly 3 months with only $6'000 income, not quite so amazing.

Almost anyone in their right mind would see an extra $10k a month from other streams of income as something to capitalise on.

This extra income steadies the ship during these kinds of Drawdown periods. Remember, the extra income can be anything that provides it, and doesn't get in the way of your trading, from a regular Job, to Commission splits, right through to conducting seminars a few times a year.

However, like we pointed out, it won't make you rich; to do that you need to keep trading. Let's look at these calculations again, but this time a few years down the line when you have a larger track record on serious money:

Trading account value $20 million

Average performance per month 2% - again this would be a very attractive return and is *probably a little on the high side*, but only your track record will tell you that for sure.

Monthly profit = $400'000

Traders performance fee = **$120'000 per month**

Suddenly we are in the realms of Ferraris every month, and nice holidays to Monaco. And the jump from $1 to $20 million isn't that spectacular. It could easily be achieved within 5 years if your record was consistent and low risk.

Now all of a sudden how does an extra $10k a month sound? Not quite as attractive but you may keep it up at a push, if you actually enjoyed the other projects that you were working on.

The point is, being a million dollar trader isn't as glamorous as it sounds, and the notion of traders having other income streams isn't such a stupid one, once you understand how the whole thing works.

When it comes to charging your fees, the industry standard is 30% performance fee. If you're trading for a fund obviously it will be lower, by the time they have taken their cut, so expect between 15 and 20% in these circumstances. As a trader you should not be doing any back office work, such as reporting to your clients. If your working on your own make sure the broker carries out these tasks on a monthly basis or that you have an assistant to do it, and if working with a fund they should have all of these features in place.

Your primary goal is to trade.

The other thing to bear in mind is that it's almost always best to trade for clients on a power of Attorney basis (POA), rather than actually taking possession of their money, in fact doing the latter puts you in the realms of illegal activity if you are not properly regulated, which is not somewhere you want to be if someone gets mad and decides to sue you.

There does comes a point though when your investors will demand that you have a fund structure in place so that they can place funds with you, this is the time that you need to look at setting up something a bit more substantial than a simple POA based trading system with a broker.

The reason is that this is simply how larger hedge funds operate; they don't have the systems to set up and track small trading accounts everywhere, so it's just easier to place large sums in one lump with another fund. To attract these kinds of investments you will obviously need your audited record on large account sizes, but you may also need to set up a separate fund to operate out of, this can be time consuming and costly, so get a professional to help you, JP Fund services are a company that im familiar with and they specialize in this kind of thing. If the cost is prohibitive, you're not ready to make that leap anyway, so just keep doing what you're doing.

At this stage you will start to meet lots of people and some of those people will be professional traders, it just happens. One of the main things that stood out to me was how few of them were actually any good. Most of them suffer the exact same issues that I did when I was sitting in front of my $200 micro account. And most of them demonstrate this with their results.

One example of this was when our broker launched a promotional event to try and locate the best fund or trader and reward them with Home page promotion on their website. We held initial meetings with the broker about our participation in the contest, and I was told that out of the 30 or so 'professional' traders and funds only about 4 were worth bothering with. The rest were basically in horrendous draw down.

I was shocked; almost 90% of the so called professionals were not even at break even, and what I found worse was the fact that they seemingly had no idea what to do about it! Shortly after this revelation, I was contacted by another broker that I had dealt with in the past, and the conversation that followed was barely believable, but so fascinating that I included it in here anyway.

The person on the other end of the line had a client, and the client had a trader that was managing his account, but unfortunately he had gotten himself into several hedges, because he didn't want to take the loss so rather than close the trades out he let them run, but placed a counter trade in the opposite direction, with the intention of closing both out at a later date, the account was down around 60%.

And the price had settled right in the middle of the two orders meaning that it was just languishing in this terrible Drawdown. The client had requested another trader to come in and assist, basically unwinding the position whilst making a series of smaller trades to put it back into profit. I was speechless; they were asking as If could just stroll into the market and make profit happen on command, as if I was harry potter or something!

This was a classic example of a private client, having warped expectations on what a professional trader is capable of, and a so called professional trader approaching the market like an idiot, Needless to say I told him I wasn't prepared to get involved and that was the last I heard of him.

The fact is, that most traders, even professionals are just people like you and I and suffer the same issues that all the other people do. This was something of a shock, as I just naturally assumed that at the top, most people would be profitable, but I was wrong.

The point of this is to help you see that there is no need to be intimidated by the fact that you are just starting out, or that you didn't come from a banking background, the fact is when trading spot currencies in a speculative fashion we all have the same chances of making or losing our money.

Apart from the fact that almost all of my preconceptions regarding fund trading and professional traders as a whole were completely wrong, there were other things that I discovered.

For example, there was the difference between retail trading environments and institutional level trading environments. This meant that while trading on a retail platform (which is what almost all retail brokers found on Google are) the prices I was looking at were not actually linked in to the Foreign exchange market proper; instead they were only *based* on the actual market. The reason for this was simply so that they could operate using fixed spreads, which in turn meant that they could offer 'no commissions' within their sales pitches.

The real live market depends on ever changing prices, provided by banks, which meant that as the various bid and offers came in, the difference between the two, commonly known as the spread, would be constantly changing within a certain range (For example EUR/USD usually tended to stay with the range of 0.5 – 2 pip spreads).

Therefore, if the broker set the spread it quoted at a constant 2 pips then, most of the time I was paying slightly too much per trade and the broker could pocket the difference, doing this meant that the broker could avoid charging direct commissions on a per trade basis, thus giving the illusion of 'Commission free trading'. This of course had obvious benefits from a marketing point of view, and depending on the spreads that they decided to set meant a larger profit margin from the actual trading their clients carried out.

However to do this they had to isolate the clients price feed from the real price feed, otherwise it would be impossible to display fixed spreads, This did of course expose the brokers to mild amounts of risk, if for example, the real spreads were much larger than the fixed amount they had set (at news times for instance) then the broker has to come up with the difference, which could be quite expensive at volatile times.

Another facet of this model was that most trades placed by clients were automatically accepted and filled, because the environment was only *based* on the live price feeds. This again exposed the broker to the risk of filling my order but then not being able to pass it onto the real market. But whilst this model gave the impression of the broker being able to manipulate prices and hunt clients stop losses, in reality this almost certainly never happened for a couple of reasons, first of all, it's quite simply in the brokers best interest to keep you trading for longer because they get all that extra spread each time you place a trade, and it would be far too much effort to monitor every stop loss placement of every single individual account, for the rewards they would be getting (a few dollars).

But how did I know all this for certain?

Quite simply, when I started trading at an institutional level, and no longer received this manufactured trading environment. As I was entering trades and taking wins and losses I started to realize that things were suddenly much different to what I was previously used to.

For example, my fills on each trade were much more complicated, and frustrating, because now, every time I entered a trade I could only get filled if there was a market participant (Bank) on the other side prepared to buy into my sells and sell into my buys at the exact same price as me, at the exact same time. Bearing in mind that the FX market is a $4 trillion a day market this doesn't sound too difficult and at small volumes it isn't, which is why the retail brokers can afford to offer you fixed spreads and guaranteed fills on your mini lot trades. However, once I was trading over 100 standard lots ($10 million each way) the fills got harder, and I started to get slippage, to the point where at least 1 or 2 pips slippage on entry and exits was expected.

No bank would fill a single trade over $1million, so the trade gets split between several banks and they all offer you slightly different fill prices.

This made a massive difference to my trading, because it resulted in not only higher cost of each trade (I needed to make 4 pips extra per trade to maintain the same performance) but it also resulted in my take profit orders not getting filled where I had set them to, or the price running slightly past my initial Stop loss levels, making my losses larger and my gains smaller in comparison.

On top of this the brokers also charge commissions on each trade placed, because at that level they are not as easily placed to show you an inflated spread, I just got what the live feed was giving me at the time.

So on top of the slippage I was experiencing each of my trades had to cover the brokers cost as well. At the time I was trading a very successful scalping strategy in which I was risking 10 pips to make 10 pips on break outs of Support and Resistance levels, this was highly compromised under these new conditions however because I wasn't getting a 1:1 risk reward I was getting a negative one instead, and as if that wasn't enough, because my stop losses were so small I had to use large amounts of leverage to achieve decent returns, which again made my trades more expensive, Over time my account would have bled to a slow and painful death, and when I realized this I knew that scalping was not the way to trade at this level, there were just too many bites being taken out of my trades on a consistent basis.

These conditions meant that I needed to trade a strategy that required far less activity, had much larger stop losses and take profits and could be traded without leverage.

I'll be honest, this was a realization I could have done with having *before* I'd started trading for a fund, but fortunately, through my helping and coaching of others I had developed several trading methods that I was able to fall back on. I could see that such a scalping strategy just wouldn't be sustainable in such a trading environment, and I stopped using it before it got me into any major trouble, other traders that I had come into contact with were not quite so far sighted, and I personally witnessed the demise of one particular trader first hand, he went from New York Shopping trips and Aston Martins to broke in under 6 months, purely because of the huge losses he incurred from scalping with too much leverage.

The main lesson from all this is that Retail trading and institutional trading are very different and what worked on your standard account may not work on large size, so If your goal is to eventually trade massive volumes, it may be worth taking these things into consideration now, and learn from the lessons that my former colleagues and I learned from the hard way.

Another option to consider is that of an ECN broker, as opposed to a dealing desk (fake environment) or a straight up institutional broker.

The difference between an ECN and a normal institutional broker is that an ECN makes everyone a liquidity provider, even you. For example, if you place a buy order, the ECN may use that order to counter a sell order placed by another trader.

This is stark contrast to a traditional institutional broker that has fixed liquidity providers, such as banks etc... With that model you are relying on those few providers filling your orders when you place them, and many times, on large size they simply won't, and you will experience greater slippage.

An ECN on the other hand, is much more flexible about using available liquidity, and therefore your trades should get filled more easily and with less slippage.

During my time trading professionally I have traded on all 3 levels and have to say that ECN offers the best type of service, particularly in terms of execution and fills. But if you trade for a fund you won't really get a choice where you trade, because that decision will be made ahead of time, over your head, you will simply have to learn the trading platform being used and get on with it.

In the end I decided that trading for a fund wasn't really for me, despite the fact that it was my dream for years and everything I had been through had been to that end. The reasons for feeling like this were two fold;

First of all the commissions were far too low to get rich particularly fast, with the structure of the fund you have too many people taking a cut of the pie, for example, out of the monthly profit generated you have to pay the IB, the Broker, the fund itself and finally, the trader.

This means that I was receiving 15% of traded profits per month.... So let's do the math once more:

Account balance $1'000'000

Monthly return 2%

Trader cut 15% = $3000

So for slaving away and suffering all the stresses that come with the territory it's quite likely that I could end up making just $3000 per month for trading a $1million account...

Even if you times the balance by 10, Im pulling in $30k per month BUT I would be generating over 200k, it just didn't seem right to me, and not really what I expected.

30k a month is a lot of money but im still not going to get rich from it, I can make as much teaching people, and I don't think that should be the case.

Plus the fact that my other trading buddies were trading their own private funds, with their own high net worth investors and they charge 50% performance fee, which is much more attractive than 15%.

I decided that the best course of action is to continue trading private clients, with a minimum account size of $250k but only if they are not ex-traders themselves, and if they sign the non contact agreements.

If trading professionally for clients is your dream, as it was mine, then I still recommend that you look at all these avenues, because out of all this I have my contacts and my reputation built up. Plus, the experience of working with other professionals in the industry is second to none and will give you far more of a stepping stone than reading this book alone, all I am trying to do is tell you how it is, or at least how it was for me, so that you can prepare accordingly, as you see fit.

Being prepared for all of these pitfalls ahead of time is gold, but being prepared for the mental challenges is something that is even more important, as we will see in the next chapter...

Resources for next level market access

www.Dukascopy.com – This broker gives very good liquidity access to the markets, and real time spreads. Their commissions are also among the most reasonable in the industry. This broker is a great introduction to institutional level trading. They are also a true ECN.

www.Cfhmarkets.com - This is a completely institutional level broker, they have no facility for retail clients whatsoever. But they offer very tight spreads (sometimes 0.5 pips on EUR/USD) and reasonable commissions. This is true market so be prepared for slippage on size.

6 PSYCHOLOGY OF PROFESSIONAL TRADING

The reason I wanted to become a professional trader was simply because I value freedom, flexibility and uncapped earning potential more than anything else including, security and comfort.

When I discovered Forex and realized that it was a business that could bring me those things I never really looked back, nor did I consider exactly how I was going to get there, I just kind of thought I would learn a strategy and trade it on money....

As we have previously looked at, trading is never that simple, because most of the time there are a hundred other things to take care of before we can just 'trade a strategy on money'. One of those things is trading psychology.

If you are telling someone that has never traded about psychology it is one of the most difficult things to explain, to them if you have some rules to follow, and those rules make money, why wouldn't you follow the rules?

To us, as traders, it's a rabbit hole that we almost deter people from jumping into.

The first psychological issues we face are the basic emotions such as fear and greed.

When I first traded for other people on a small scale I was terrified to place a trade in case it lost, this kept my risk low which was positive, but it also impeded my ability to actually make a profit which was bad.

The other side to that coin is greed or revenge trading, and while I have always been naturally good at switching off my emotional attachment to money, I have met and worked closely with other traders that have not, which has been one of the most fascinating and mind blowing experiences of my trading career thus far...

I remember right after I had taken on a few private accounts, I met a couple of other traders in my local area through trading forums and they were, in my mind, slightly ahead of me in terms of experience and size of funds traded, but they were still trading either private accounts or their own pots.

Because I thought it would be good experience to mix with these guys on a daily basis, I suggested that we rent a local office space, and trade together for the London session.

They agreed and we moved our stuff in and began trading our respective accounts.

For a start, I felt way behind in terms of equipment, these guys had multiple monitor displays, expensive computer equipment and subscriptions to price and order feeds that I never even heard of. Looking back I must have looked like a total amateur with my laptop and free charting software.

As the weeks went by I witnessed things that would never forget and use as a lesson to myself from that day forward.

One particular day, we were discussing the concept different brokers of commission splits and I suggested that they sign up to my broker at the time (Dukascopy) because I had a very good relationship with them, and could probably get them a better deal on their spreads, so they agreed and made the switch.

In return for this I got a split of their commissions from the broker each time they placed a trade, which I gave half of back to the traders, so everyone was a winner.

Several days later, one of the traders got into a position just before a major news event, and by the time the event came out and the price rocketed against his position his fill was not honored, due to the massive amounts of liquidity pushing the markets only one way, there was simply no one else to fill his order at that price. This was to be the start of events that would result in a series of revenge trades, a £100'000 loss and a massive bonus for me in terms of commissions!

The initial slippage cost him quite a few pips, but it wasn't a total disaster, but in the moment he decided to place a trade in the aftermath of the announcement, in the direction that the market was heading, it lost, so he assumed it was a retracement and that now it had pulled back he would get back in.... He lost again.

With each new trade there was less and less rationalization behind the entry and more and more leverage used to claw back his previous losses, as an IB for his account, I was privy to the account statements and could basically watch all of this unfold quietly on the other side of the room.

This went on for 2 or 3 hours until he had lost over £100'000 (Almost $200'000 at the time)

He was absolutely devastated and a total mess, to the point of being physically ill and the account he was trading had suffered massive damage. I personally witnessed him get sucked into a black hole of revenge trading and it was not pretty. I decided right there in that room that whatever I did, I would never do that, I would rather have my steady smooth losses associated with switching and keeping risk tight than that.

At the end of the month I received almost $6000 in commissions delivered straight into my bank account, it was a bitter sweet feeling, knowing it came as a direct result of my good friend being totally fried. I took him for lunch.

However we try and cover our angles, the psychology of trading will get us somehow, even more so when we desire to trade large funds, as I was about to discover.

Up to the point of trading for the fund, I had never really experienced any kind of emotions in my trading and certainly not to those extremes, but then again I had never really traded large size either...

My time came when I was allocated an account worth just around $70'000 as a starting point with the fund. I calculated my risk and I was to trade around 3 standard lots. For some reason that I can't fully explain to this day when I came to place my first trade on the account, I froze, and literally couldn't do it, the fear was extreme.

This was ridiculous; we are talking about $30 per pip, it was nothing really, but to me it was insane, and I was physically ill just attempting to trade those levels, considering my dream, I thought that my career as a trader was over.

But after a few weeks, and a few trades placed I was fine and never looked back, to the point where just a few months later I was trading much larger accounts and pumping $10 million orders into the market on a daily basis, and no other size affected me like the time I jumped to 3 standard lots.

Traders call this the 'mental block level' and it's the point at which your brain basically gets freaked out by the cash value of your trading. It only occurs once, and once you are past it, rarely happens again.

All I can say is that it can be any value level from 5 mini lots up to 50 standard lots depending on the trader but you will know when you hit it, and to just trade through it until you are back to normal, which is obviously easier said than done, but possible.

This was one of the strangest and least expected psychological events in my trading adventure, and to this day it baffles me.

As my knowledge of the basics developed and I started getting into a position where I could find a strategy, place a trade, manage the trade and exit the trade, this is when the psychological issues really began to take hold of me and drastically increase the time it took me to become consistently profitable.

Many people never release the negative grip that trading psychology has over them and from my own experience, the main reason is that they can't see how its effecting them directly at the time, so it slowly undermines all of their efforts until they are either broke or give up and go back to 'reality'.

The problem is that you can hardly ever identify the problems as you go; it's only with hind sight that they become clear and patterns emerge.

The first real issue on the road to trading a fund for me was that of Recency bias, which is basically where your brain tells you how you're feeling based on the most recent events, which is how almost all human brains operate.

So from a trading point of view, you could have been profitable all month, then on the last few days you lose every trade you take... this results in a negative mind set, because the most recent results have been negative (despite all your initial success)

Recency bias is basically built into all of us, and it's not just applicable to trading, but trading is one of those exercises that perfectly allows the effects to take charge and causes one of the most debilitating trading weaknesses, that we have all been through at some point, switching.

Switching is where you stop trading a system because it 'stopped working'.

From my experience of knowing other professional traders, working with funds and trader coaching it is without doubt the number one cause of traders to lose all their money, just ahead of overleveraging, and I will explain why...

If you are trading an account with a system that you have found or built, then, as we have previously mentioned, the cycle goes a little something like this; lightly back test the system and decide it's amazing, then proceed to trade it on your account, take several losses until your balance is slightly negative from when you started and dump the system as ineffective... Continue this cycle several times with different systems and what you get is an equity curve that smoothly falls until you stop trading or run out of money.

When you think about it logically, and with hind sight, it's obvious and makes perfect sense, if you only trade a system until it loses then swap to another one and repeat that cycle all you can ever do is lose money with this method of operation, trading really is a mugs game and you are the king of mug town.

However, when you are in the moment, swapping and finding a 'better strategy' actually makes logical sense, after all why would you continue to trade something that loses?

This seems like the ultimate contradiction, but as we previously learned when you understand the nature of trading it makes perfect sense. The fact is that trading is not investing, it's a game, like roulette and just like roulette it's a game of odds and probabilities.

This means that, just like any other game of odds and probabilities the outcome of the next trade has nothing to do with the outcome of the last trade or even any supposed 'odds' that may be associated with that game.

Another example is flipping a coin.

We all know that flipping a coin carries a 50 / 50 chance of getting a heads or a tails, however, if you flip a coin 10 times you will very rarely get 5 heads and 5 tails, why?

Because just like roulette and trading anything can happen on a small sample of flips, in fact it's not out of the question to get a whole sample of 10 heads or 10 tails; this is simply the nature of these types of games.

Now try flipping a coin 100 times or more, and you should see a much smoother outcome overall, but in those 100 flips there will still be instances of 10 heads or tails in a row etc...

The more flips you record the closer the outcome overall will be to your expected odds (50%)

The fewer amounts of flips you take the more erratic the performance becomes and the more likely you are to experience results far away from your expected outcome based on the odds.

Let's go back to roulette and the reason casinos stay in business:

Roulette is also a game of odds and probabilities, however, with roulette the odds are ever so slightly in favor of the casino. The results are almost the same.

You can walk into a casino and take 10 bets on red or black and lose each one, even though you are 'supposed' get roughly half of them in your favor. Equally you can go into another casino and make a fortune on those same 10 bets.

The casino only makes money from you because you keep betting, and the more bets you place the more the odds play out as expected, which in this case means that the casino wins ever so slightly more than you, taking all of your money and everyone else's in the process.

Hence over sustained betting the house always wins.

Now come back to trading, with the mind-set that it also is a game of odds and probabilities.

Remember, anything can happen on each trade because there are a hundred things affecting the market in each moment that may not be there in the next moment, and the large traders moving the market are almost certainly not looking at the same set up that you are, in fact, all we are trying to do is look for price patterns that tell us when these large market movers might be about to make their next push on the market, and get in on the right side just before they do.

Now bear in mind that because we are just trading with odds, the fewer trades we take, the more erratic the results will be compared to our expectations. This explains those times when you start trading a strategy and it loses 4 or 5 times in a row.

This is normal because you have only taken a few trades, to get the edge that you have to play out for you; you need to trade over a sustained period of time, only then will the system prove profitable on a consistent basis.

But when you switch you never ever give the edge time to play out in your favor and worse still, swap only when the results are negative.

If you go back over every strategy you have ever used and ditched I can almost guarantee that many of them will actually work over a sustained period of trading, but you simply didn't give them a chance to.

By the time I started trading my first clients account I was using a basic moving average crossover technique, which in my first month saw me take 4% out of the market, I was happy. By the end of the third month I was trading a completely different system, simply because I had experienced a losing streak, and my expectations were skewed.

Needless to say my equity curve slowly and smoothly dropped over the next few months until I stopped trading and evaluated what was going on. And the simple fact of the matter was, I had been switching to a loss and therefore losing.

I can almost guarantee that this is something you have been experiencing if you analyze the past 6 months of your personal trading honestly. The good news is that you probably have a lot of strategies at hand that you can test and trade with.

This time of switching did help me develop my skill that I am pleased to have today, and that is the ability to create brand new systems from scratch and using almost no indicators.

This came in particularly useful when I needed to change from the scalping strategy to something more fund friendly.

The good news is that now you understand why every strategy will go through a losing streak, and that if you test and prove it properly you can make consistent profits, you will find it much easier to identify and overcome the dreaded Recency bias... the bad news is that is only the start of the psychological issues.

Most new traders never make it past Recency bias with the switching and thus never actually experience the other psychological killers of trading, it's kind of like being stuck at the second hurdle and not being able to see over the other side. However, if you do ever make it past that one, the next one is even harder to overcome, and ten times more subversive.

The next hurdle I encountered was that of self sabotage.

This is such a poisonous, hidden issue that it is extremely easy to completely miss it, and allow it to constantly hold your trading back until you basically give up.

Self sabotage explains those bizarre moments in your life when you just know that taking a certain course of action will result in getting you closer to your goal, but for some reason your own mind constantly stops you doing it, either by distracting you with other things or coming up with 'reasons' why you can't do it just at the moment.

It is extremely difficult to explain, but if you have ever looked back and wondered why you did what you actually did instead of what you know you should have done, self sabotage is your problem.

How does this affect our trading?

Again, as with so many of my revelations in this business, and more so in the realms of trading psychology, my various roles and experiences, not only as a fund trader but also as someone who has worked with and trained hundreds of people allows me to watch for the common patterns, relate them to myself and then identify them as something worth noting and overcoming.

I first realized how damaging self sabotage was after witnessing it in lots of my students that I was teaching.

There would be a fair few traders that I would coach through the Recency bias problem, and they would come out the other side, consistently profitable and in a much stronger position than when I first met them. However many of these 'success stories' would go on to completely undo all of their previous hard work and almost go right back to square one with their trading.

If I hadn't witnessed it dozens of times over and over again, in an almost predictable pattern with my students I probably would hardly have noticed it, even though I myself was affected by it at one time. It's a very similar concept to switching, because you get so caught up in the act of finding a strategy that works, you fail to step back and realize that it's the switching that is killing your account.

Self Sabotage is very similar because you get so caught up with worrying that your strategy might stop working or that your performance isn't as good as it should be you start focusing on ways to make it better, switch, or just go mentally insane.

It is one of the main reasons why it took me so long to actually write this book, there would always be a distraction or a 'reason' for me not to do it, and procrastinate, despite knowing that a book like this would be extremely interesting to many aspiring traders who have the same dream in the beginning, not to mention helpful to my own career, being a published author in such a niche, sought after area.

Self sabotage has stopped me testing and proving strategies that have shown extremely great promise, developing training material that I know would be extremely unique and helpful to other traders and starting a whole host of other businesses outside of trading.

It is also the reason that I have a pile of FSA registration forms on my desk right now, that I haven't filled out yet because iv 'been busy' even though I am fully aware that my track record combined with being fully, independently regulated by a major government agency will gain me access to millions of pounds worth of investment and immense amounts of credibility among my investors.... Sigh.

I remember one student of mine had just completed the testing of a strategy as I coached him to do, and he was doing extremely well, then he wrote to me one day expressing grave concerns at his performance and how worried he was that his strategy might not be working, and he wasn't sure what to do.

This sounded strange because I knew he was doing everything right and I couldn't imagine that his strategy would just stop working a few weeks later, so I asked him to send me his data, and his account statements so that I could get a better idea of what was going on.

It turned out that nothing had really changed in terms of his performance, except he had had a few losses recently, but nothing that wasn't to already be expected from his strategy, I remember also showing his data (With his permission) to a group of students that I was coaching at the time, to get their unbiased take on what they were looking at.

Almost every single trader wanted to know more about his strategy and how he was achieving such fantastic returns, and everyone was in agreement that this was the kind of consistency they dreamt of achieving.

When he saw their reactions he couldn't believe it, and was instantly encouraged to continue on in his course and develop his trading further. Needless to say his success continued.

The point which became apparent is that your mind makes you see or feel what it wants you to feel despite the cold hard facts staring you in the face, so irrespective of the fact you want to succeed, if you don't feel that you deserve it or that you should be doing it right now, your subconscious mind will always find ways of blocking your access to your goals.

On way to overcome this is to surround yourself with other traders, that you can bounce things off, so that when you feel like you're not performing, get their opinions, and most times you will be surprised.

Another way to help with Self sabotage is to form a plan, in writing, of how you will achieve your goal, step by step, and follow the plan religiously. This helps keep you on track and stop distractions throwing you off course.

Once you overcome the basic emotions, Recency bias and self sabotage you are basically limitless in what you can achieve in your trading.

Many of these things you don't discover until you are in the moment or past them, so hopefully this book can prepare you for the psychological journey ahead, and help you live the journey as an adventure rather than a burden.

7 STEP BY STEP PLAN TO FUND TRADING

If you dream of trading millions, and working with institutional investors and traders of a like mind, then you really do need a plan.

This is the one thing I never really had, because as we have already mentioned most of the things I learned, could only have been learned by actually doing them and getting past them, or by reading a handy book that someone who has been through that process has written.

Sadly for me, I didn't have that book, so the whole thing took me much longer and cost me way more in terms of money and emotional stress.

This chapter is meant to simply give you a direct guide to what you need to do in a step by step fashion, and hopefully you will get where I got much faster.

Step 1 - Learn your niche

You're a currency trader, so absorb as much as you can in the way of education on trading the markets. This does not mean buying lots of expensive courses or seminars, because most people running these things have no idea about any of the pitfalls and hurdles that you will face as a professional trader, they have likely never made it past the first hurdle of basic emotions, and if they have they almost certainly never got past Recency bias and switching. All they can teach you are the basic emotional issues, and technical analysis.

This does mean, <u>practice.</u>

Spend time in front of the charts and learn to recognize price patterns that you can formulate into a strategy and test before going live, live and breathe these patterns and you will become an expert in them, over time.

This process could take 6 months or 2 years depending on what strategies you are looking at, but 2 years of inching progress is much better than 5 years of going in circles and losing money.

Step 2 – Find your broker, build your track record

The next step once you have your method of trading nailed, trade it!

Like we looked at, find a broker that is aware of your goals, make sure they will help you when the time is right, if you have to become an IB for them and introduce a few trading buddies to get them sweet. This combined with your live trading should encourage them to open some doors later on.

If you want to trade your own clients, via power of attorney then make sure they have those capabilities, or if you are looking for some connections to existing funds, again make sure they have those kinds of clients on board.

At the same time register your trading account somewhere online, such as myfxbook.com, so that your performance can be tracked and verified; also take the time to locate some companies to do this later on. If your account is small then look for a local CPA that is willing to certify your trading results for you, When it comes to verification, *anything is better than nothing*.

This should take around 12 months of good solid trading.

Step 3 - Build up your contact lists, credibility and exposure

Basically when the time is right you want a network of established industry professionals that know you and inclined to help you. They must also be aware that you are a golden goose who will make them money with your trading.

It's important to build up your networks before and while you are building your track record, as this creates trust and credibility. If you just popped out of the blue one day people are less likely to help you. But if you know your contact at the broker well, and have spoken to a couple of funds and have a blog or website where you regularly post you trades and help newer traders overcome their problems you will have massive credibility.

Not to mention the fact that you will be exposing yourself to opportunities.

I heard a saying once that I loved, luck is simply preparation and opportunity coming together. So if you want to get 'lucky' get prepared and create as many opportunities as you can.

LinkedIn is a fantastic site, it's like the face-book of the business world, and you can almost guarantee that your contacts are already on there, so join up!

Write a book, offer to speak at local universities or colleges about trading for free, and submit articles to popular trading magazines or websites, anything that cements your status as an expert should be considered.

Step 4 - Create your image

Once you have your proven track record and a bank of contacts in the industry, it's time to put them all together and make some serious money.

Build a website, hire a virtual assistant to handle enquiries in a professional looking manner, and create offline material such as brochures for your trading.

Your clients should be signing professional looking Power of attorney forms, non contact agreement policies, and client agreements. Everything should appear proper and professional, and most importantly branded with your company logo and that of the broker you are using.

All of this looks competent and trust worthy, and will be congruent with your proven track record, there is nothing worse than a 'successful currency trader' who made excellent returns last year, turning up to a investor meeting on the bus with no literature, and cheap clothes.

People have a certain image of a currency trader, and you need to be that image, both with your actual trading performance and your overall appearance.

Step 5 - Start trading

This might seem simple and logical, but it must be done as part of an overall plan similar to the one I have given you here.

Trust me if you go into this whole thing unprepared, you are in for a rough ride, and if you do make it, you will have definitely took the long way around.

However, if you do it properly and plan everything from the very start there is nothing that can hold you back and the truth is that with the appropriate preparation, the easiest part to this whole thing is finding money to trade.

People are naturally greedy; this is why so many of them find themselves on the end of a scam or fraud. It may sound Machiavellian, but you can use this fact to your advantage.

When you can genuinely offer them verified, above average returns, and a credible, professional image all you need to do is give a good sales pitch and they will be eating out of your hand!

Here is a list of advantages that a currency trading account offers for the individual investor:

- Flexibility; they can close it and withdraw their money at any time with just a few hours notice
- Above average returns
- Complete security of their funds; Traders have no access to their money, which means they can't steal it, and some brokers, namely Dukascopy, allow their clients to keep their money in an actual bank account too, and the banks they use are not small either, including the likes of Barclays and Merrill lynch.
- All returns are verified by an independent third party

In fact many people call a successfully managed Forex account the perfect investment for the obvious benefits over any other type of instrument on the market.

Once you have your first seed capital in place, and do well on this for your clients and broker to witness, the whole business will become a snowball effect and your fund will grow exponentially.

I have indeed lived my dream thus far, and achieved what I wanted to at the beginning of my adventure.

Looking back I have made many mistakes, and met some fascinating people and ultimately had my whole perception of professional trading turned on its head. The fact is that the people at the 'top' don't really know any more than the people at the bottom, they are all just battling their human emotions and trying to find and profit from their niche in the markets.

I have seen so called professional traders, managing millions, make serious errors that I wouldn't have even considered making on my first demo account, but I have also met some very successful people that inspire me to keep pursuing my dream until I make it.

The other curious fact I discovered, is that when you are firmly on your journey your 'dream' will alter and change many times, based on your experiences as you go, and that is a good thing because usually the dream becomes grander and slightly more elusive, and this is what keeps you going through all of those tough times, draw downs and criticisms.

Trading a currency fund is fun, exciting and terrifying, because nothing can prepare you for trading at that kind of level, no matter how much you practice, at some point you have to push the button on a trade that will pump millions of Dollars into the market, and maybe, one day, even more.

By the age of 26 I had travelled the world, and worked in more countries and with more people than I care to remember, I have lived in luxury apartments on the beach, trading from my laptop, I have flown to the other side of the world just for the weekend, to meet with fellow traders and colleagues, I have lived in cities and places that most people only dream of visiting for a few days, and all of this, everything, has been possible only through trading Forex online.

You may decide that after reading this it's not for you, and you would prefer to remain in your job or working your other business which gives you that much cherished security.

But if you have at least a shred of curiosity, or doubt as to whether you should go down this road, then my advice is to do it, make sure you plan and do it right, but ultimately it will be an experience you will never forget!

ABOUT THE AUTHOR

Jarratt Davis began his Forex adventure in 2005 after selling his off line businesses. He ventured into Forex because he wished to travel the world without ruining his chances of a career later on. He began trading for the WealthbuilderFX hedge fund in 2008 and coaching and mentoring less experienced traders in 2009.

He currently travels the world, and has lived in many countries including the UK, Spain, Switzerland, Canada, the US and the Canary Islands.
He regularly conducts seminars and speaking engagements on the process of becoming a profitable trader from a non related back ground, and contributes to many industry events and publications.

His website is www.JarrattDavis.com

19041385R00055

Made in the USA
Lexington, KY
04 December 2012